DEDICATION

This book is dedicated to all the family and friends that were and are entrepreneurs. People that have made the extra effort to Ensure that they control their own lives. From my Grandparents who were entrepreneurs and had their own businesses to my nephews that I am certain that their desire to have Their own money will also become entrepreneurs. It has been the limitless support from my family that has enabled me to make my life my own.

These people have always encouraged Me to walk to the beat of my own drum.

DRUM BEATS

WE ALL HAVE OUR OWN BEATS THAT ONLY WE CAN HEAR

IT IS ALSO WHAT PEOPLE FEEL WHEN THEY COME NEAR

OUR BEATS ARE WHAT DEFINES US, WHAT MAKES US WHO WE ARE

IT'S WHEN WE TRY AND CHANGE THEM AT THE REQUEST OF OTHERS

THAT WE FEEL THE SAME PAIN AS BEING HIT BY A CAR

THOSE THAT ALL MARCH TO THE SAME BEAT

ALL STUMBLE AND FALL WHEN ONE SINGLE PERSON TRIPS OVER THEIR OWN FEET

IT SOMETIMES TROUBLES US BECAUSE NO ONE ELSE HEARS IT

WE ASK IS IT US OR IS IT THEM WHEN WE TRY TO UNDERSTAND WHY

BECAUSE IT IS IMPORTANT FOR US TO FIT IN SO WE CAN ALL LAUGH AND CRY

I HAVE LEARNED THAT THE BEAT THAT I HEAR IS MY VERY OWN AND AM NOW HAPPY THAT NO ONE ELSE HEARS IT

SO I WHEN I HEAR IT I KNOW THAT I AM HOME

WHAT I CAN DO IS COMBINE MY BEATS WITH THE OTHERS THAT I HEAR

TO CREATE A BRAND NEW SOUND TOGETHER THAT WE ALL CAN ENJOY AND LISTEN TO ALL AS ONE WITHOUT FEAR

PAPIM-2012

PAPI-M-THOUGHTS.BLOGSPOT.COM

CONTENTS

2

INTRODUCTION

Why I wrote this book. I have been a consultant for over 20 years helping people all over the world start and run their own businesses. I have helped people start successful for-profit and non-profit businesses. I started working on this book by listing the questions that people ask me the most. What I came to realize is that many people started working on their business plans and/or taking training with little progress forward and became frustrated with the whole process.

What I came to realize were two important points,

One

A great number of people lacked the confidence to get things started. They didn't think they had what it takes to work on their own. Surprisingly a lot did not think they had the education and background to launch and sustain a successful business.

Two

Most people jumped right into starting their business without taking the time to work on developing their business ideas. Most did not do the research and development to see if their ideas would work before investing money in training and setting up the business.

As I was developing the book I realized that my entrepreneurial training came from decades of people in my own family running their own successful businesses. We sometimes forget things that we learned as a child that are still with us today. I remember at age 10 my father taking me to find my first job. Then it was a series of paper routes, door to door sales, cutting grass and many other ways that I came up with to make my own money. My brother even recalls working for me, although I think I paid him with ice cream versus real money.

This book will help you figure out how to evaluate your business idea and create an action plan to get you into business.

Thanks for buying my book and Yes You Can Start Your Own Business!

Marc Parham

YES I CAN – DEVELOP MY BUSINESS IDEA AND START MY OWN BUSINESS

Written by Marc E. Parham, Business Development Consultant, Partec Consulting Group,
marcp@partecgroup.com, www.partecgroup.com,

Developing Your Business Idea

- ➲ Have you been thinking about starting a small business but are not sure where to begin?
- ➲ Do you have a business idea that you want to develop?
- ➲ Have you come up with a product idea that you want to bring to market?
- ➲ Do you have a hobby or something that you already have been doing to make money and want to turn it into a small business?

If you answered YES to any of these questions

THIS BOOK IS FOR YOU!

This book and the accompanying exercises will help you answer the basic questions to evaluate if your business idea can make you money. These questions are the basic questions that you will have to ask and answer as you move down the path of starting your business. They are by no means all the questions that you will need to answer but they will help you to begin to put yourself into the right mindset to move your business idea forward.

More people today have decided they want to their own small business. Some have decided because of a passion that they have always had others because of the current un-employment situation.

Regardless the reason, many people have decided that it is time to take their ideas to action and start their own a business or organization.

This book will guide you through how to ask and do the research to answer these questions in a way that makes sense to you. Upon completion of this book and the associated exercises you will have a good understanding of how to develop a business plan for your business idea.

The purpose of this book is that you will learn how research and develop your business ideas and then take your Ideas to action to start your business.

The Basic Questions

1. Am I self-motivated and do I have the right mind set?
2. Why should I start a business?
3. Am I ready to start a business?
4. Do I need a business plan?
5. What are the most important task that I should focus on before I start my business?
6. What do I sell?
7. Who will be my customers? Who will be my competition?
8. How much should I charge?
9. How much will it cost me to start my business?
10. How do I develop my business idea?
11. How do I create an action plan to start my business?
12. How do I put it all together?

The Goal of This Book

This book was designed to help you develop your business idea by breaking down the different aspects of developing a business idea into small individual segments. Once all segments have been completed the information can be used to develop a strategic business plan for your business.

You will be able to use the information to do the following;

- To give you a better idea of what it will take for you to start and run your business
- To use as a foundation to develop a business plan
- To have discussions with potential investors or funders about your idea
- To do focus group or other forms of market research to test your idea

BOOK ORGANIZATION

This book contains the following features:

- **The Main Book** – This book contains the questions and discussions about the items described in the contents.
- **Do This!** – After most sections in the book there will be a sidebar labeled **"Do This!"** This sidebar contains exercises that as you complete them, will help you develop your idea.
- **Online Tools** – The surveys, templates, and other tools necessary to complete the "Do This!" are located on the **Small Business Capacity Builder** website where you can download or take surveys online. You will be emailed the results of any survey that you take online to add to the information that will be used to develop your idea.
- **Small Business Capacity Builder Website** – This is a Capacity Builder Network site that contains articles, resources, online training and other important information. You can post questions and discussions about topics that are of interest to you.
- By purchasing this book you will receive the **password** to do the assigned work.
- You are encouraged to create your own user profile as the first step in preparation for doing the exercises.

Before we began working on developing a new business idea I think it is important to have the right mindset. Please review the topics below that will help you get into the **right mindset**.

Are you self-motivated?

Do you have the right mindset?

SMALL BUSINESS REVISITED!

Remember when your parents, uncles, aunts, relatives and other friends had more than one job. One of my uncles worked on cars and my grandmother did hair and other people did a variety of things to make money.

They had a main job that they did during the day or night and then had something else that they did on the weekends and other free time.

We have always been small businesspersons. We have always used our skills to take care of our families.

Within the last few years something has changed!

- ➲ People have been told that they only need an education, a job, a house, and a car and they will be living the American dream.

- ➲ A dream that has been recently shattered by the current economic situation. People have done what they were told and now are losing everything that they worked so hard to get.

Do This! – (1)
Entrepreneurship Family Tree

Objective:

Create a short list of family members and friends that have had a business or activity the generated legal revenue.

Activity:

Use the form in the **Do This** Section to create a list of the first 4 people that you feel have been able to successfully generate money running a business or performing a specific activity.

Instructions: Page 36

○ They worked so hard for someone else!

○ The same someone who when the times got hard, took the money and literarily ran.

It is time to get back to the things that made this country what it once was, people working for themselves, working together to create a safe and secure life for their families.

> I remember growing up that my father always had something else going on. He worked as a hospital administrator during the day but on the weekends and some nights he was a janitor at some of the high schools in the area. He would take my brother and I with him to work to help out. We thought it was fun. Had I known something about child labor laws back then I would have asked for a piece of the action, but knowing him he would have said "you know that pork chop that you ate last night for dinner? Consider yourself paid in full"

Small Businessperson or Entrepreneur?

There are many ways that people determine who is a small business person and who is an entrepreneur. You will find that people will spend a great deal of time debating over what the difference is. For the sake of getting you through this book I will list the definitions and you can figure where you fit, but the most important thing to consider about both definitions is that;

○ They both end up with a person taking the steps necessary to utilize their skills, knowledge and experience to create a business that produces revenue that they can use to take care of their responsibilities and control their lives.

> An **entrepreneur** (🔊 /ˌɒntrəprəˈnɜr/) is an enterprising individual who builds capital through risk and/or initiative.[1][note 1] The term was originally a loanword from French and was first defined by the Irish-French economist Richard Cantillon. This term first appeared in the French Dictionary "Dictionnaire Universal de Commerce" of Jacques des Bruslons published in 1723. Entrepreneur in English is a term applied to a person who is willing to help launch a new venture or enterprise and accept full responsibility for the outcome. Source: http://en.wikipedia.org/wiki/Entrepreneur

What constitutes a **small business** varies widely around the world. Small businesses are normally privately owned corporations, partnerships, or sole proprietorships. What constitutes "small" in terms of government support and tax policy varies by country and by industry, ranging from fewer than 15 employees under the Australian _Fair Work Act 2009_, 50 employees in the European Union, and fewer than 500 employees to qualify for many U.S. Small Business Administration programs, although in 2006 there were over 18,000 "small businesses" with over 500 employees that accounted for half of all the employees employed by all "small business ". [1] [2] Small businesses can also be classified according to other methods such as sales, assets, or net profits. Source: http://en.wikipedia.org/wiki/Small_business

A few ideas to consider….

✓ **You may already have your own small business!**

➲ Do you have a hobby or something that you like to do that others have paid you to do for them?

➲ If you have a job and someone is paying you to do work for them, you actually have your own small business. It doesn't matter what you do but you do provide a product or service that someone is paying you for. You just don't do any of the marketing, accounting, or the management of the business. You do the work and the business takes care of the rest.

➲ We sometimes take for granted the basic skills that we use to do our jobs. We sometimes don't realize that even the most basic job requires a specific set of skills that can sometimes be transferred to another job or business.

  ✓ For example, we might have a job as a janitor for a company. In order to do our job effectively we have to use the basic skills of;

  • **Time management** – If there is a whole building or floor to clean we must know how much time to spend in each area to get all of the work done in the time allotted.

  • **Tools and Equipment** – we have to know what cleaners to use on which surfaces and what tools to use to do the best job.

✓ You are not in this alone!

You're not in this alone! There are many people just like you that are looking to start their own businesses. There are a number of organizations that are here to help you achieve your goal of the starting your own business.

✓ You must have dedication and passion!

You must have dedication and passion if you plan to be successful in this business. This has to be something that you would do if money were not the issue. It will not be easy but if you dedicate yourself and have passion you will be successful.

✓ You must develop and follow a plan!

The most important thing is that you must develop and follow plan. Nothing more to say about this.

And...Yes You Can Do This!

2. Why should I start my own business?

The real question is, why should I did not start my own business? Most employers have had to cut costs due to rising cost of having employees. Health Insurance plans, taxes and employee related overhead, cost a lot for a business. This is especially important for small business. If you were a business owner would you not do the same?

The unemployment rate is high. This means a lot of people with skills do not have jobs. Where have all the jobs gone?

▸ **What if, a business could use your service or skill without having to pay all the additional cost?**

▸ **What if, multiple businesses used your skill or service without having to pay all the additional cost?**

You are the product!

Any job that you have worked at as an employee, you were the product. The work that you did on your job you were paid for by your employer. I don't care what you did. You provided a service and were paid for that service. *The only difference is that you let the business get all of the financial benefits by not making you worry about how the business worked.*

A sweet deal until they decide they don't need your product any longer!

Can every job be converted to a business? I have to say the answer is no, not every job, but you will be surprised to learn that most of the time, the skills that you learned and applied can be used in another business to do something else.

Think about it.

➲ If you had multiple businesses/customers/clients buying your product at the same time, losing one of them might not affect your cash flow in a major way.

This is what business is all about!

20 Home-based business ideas!

Webpreneur	Consultant
Housesitter / Petsitter	Professional Organizer
Independent Sales Representative	Personal Services - Shopping & Errands
Desktop Publishing	Tutoring
eBay Seller	Home day care
Yard work	Computer maintenance
Recycler	Cleaning service
Virtual assistant	Remote bookkeeper
Translator	Health insurance consultant
Elder assistant	Copywriter

3. Am I ready to start my own business?

Do you have a skill that people will pay to use? Do you have a hobby that people will pay you to do for them? Do you have a new idea that will make life easier for people?

For example, you've been a painter for the last 10 years. You do great work and you have been doing it for other people. They find the jobs, you do the work, they get paid, and then they pay you.

Why can't you find the jobs, you make sure the work gets done, you get paid, and then you pay you!

That sounds a lot better doesn't it?

Another example; Dana really likes scrapbooking. She does it for herself, her family and her friends. Everyone likes how she does it. People are always saying I wish I could do that. Dana could set up classes to teach people how to do it. For those who don't want to it do for themselves she could do for them, for a price.

One more example; Kevin is great at cutting grass. He takes pride in his work and has worked for many landscape companies over the years. He even cuts his friends and neighbors yards because he likes to do it. They offer to pay him but he really doesn't accept it. He maybe accepts a burger off the grill or a glass of lemonade.

Do This! – (2)
Self -Assessment

Objective:

Do a self-assessment of yourself to determine your readiness to start a business.

Activity:

Use the **Self-Assessment** form in this book, or take the online Self-Assessment on the Small Business Capacity Builder website.

Instructions: Page 38

The fact is, if they're not doing it themselves,
They are paying someone to do it.
Why Not You!

Most people feel that a startup business has to replace their income. This is not true! Starting a home base business while you have income is the best way to do it. It will give you the opportunity to generate additional income in your spare time.

People come to me all the time and say that in order for them to be successful in business they need to pay all their bills right from the start. I tell them to focus on paying one bill at a time. Say your phone bill is $200 per month. Try and set a goal to make enough money to pay the phone bill for a few months. Then add on another bill, then another, then another. Before long you end up paying all your bills. To me, that is the beginning of a successful business.

What if you don't have any income? This is a case for many people today. They have skills, they have a willingness to work, but they don't have jobs.

Why not create your own job? Develop a business around something you like to do that people are already paying someone else to do or sell a product that someone needs and will pay for.

With the way things are right now, most of us don't have the time to do some of the most basic task like cutting grass, painting, and even cooking a healthy meal. You would be surprised what people will pay to make their lives a little easier.

4. Do I need a business plan?

Let's see. You decide that you'd like to build a home entertainment center but you've never done it before. You have an idea in your mind what you want it to look like. You buy the wood, you buy the nails, and you buy all the other supplies you think you will need. Now you start to work. You start cutting and nailing. You work for days. You use up all the wood and then have to go buy more.☹ You keep working and working but it never looks like what you saw in your mind.

<table>
<tr><td rowspan="8">

Do This! - (3)

Review Sample Business Plans

Objective:

Search for and review sample businesses plans for your business ideas.

Activity:

Go to www.bplans.com and search their large database of sample business plans.

Instructions: Page 41

</td></tr>
</table>

What did not have been easier if you have a plan?

You need something to guide you through the process.

That's what a business plan is. This is why you need one.

Your business plan describes these important things

- ✓ What type of business you are starting?
- ✓ Why you decided to start it,
- ✓ What you are going to sell,
- ✓ Who you are going to sell it to,
- ✓ How much are you going to charge for what you are selling?
- ✓ How you are going to finance your business
- ✓ How you're going to operate your business so that it remains successful.

One question that I get a lot is "Can you write my business plan for me?" I immediately say "No I can't, but I can help you write your own business plan. " Writing your own plan is very important. How do you expect people to help or fund you once they realize that you could not even put together your own plan for running your business? The plan is there, I just have to help you get it out of your head and onto paper.

5. What are the first things I should do before I start my own business?

The first three steps before starting a business are;

1. Research!
2. Research!
3. Research!

The internet makes it very easy to research any business idea. Unless you come up with something very special, someone else has done what you're trying to do. There are tons of web sites, articles, electronic books and videos that contain very useful information. You can find sample business plans and web sites similar to the company that you are thinking about starting.

You're not good we using the computer? Then find someone that is. You could probably even find a young person like your son or daughter to do the research for you.

The point I am trying to make is, THE RESEARCH MUST BE DONE!

One of the most important things that you have to remember is to bookmark the sites that contain information that you want to go back to.

Let me give you a short sample of how one might research a business idea;

Let's continue with the previous example using Kevin who enjoys cutting grass.

1. Kevin is thinking about starting his own landscaping business. He's been working for other companies for a while so he kind of understands how the business works.

2. He wants to make sure that he doesn't spend too much money on gas so he wants to work close to where he lives. Kevin can get on the Internet, open a global search window and enter in the search field, "landscape companies, his zip code" (landscape companies, 30033).

3. Any landscape company that has a web site and is located in his zip code will be displayed. Kevin can now click on each web site to do research on what services they offer, pricing and so they do business. After reviewing only a few sites he will get a better understanding of his competition and what he might do to get his share of the market.

4. In a short time Kevin has gained a lot of very useful information. Using the Internet to do research is one of the quickest ways to get the information you need.

Do This!-(4)

Research Your Business Idea

Objective:

Learn how to use simple search terms to research your business ideas.

Activity:

Use Google to research businesses similar to the one you would like to start.

Instructions: Page 42

When doing research on the Internet I will open a blank document in Microsoft Word or another word processor and cut and paste interesting items that I find to save for later reading. I find that it is sometimes difficult to research and deeply read at the same time. I will cut and paste all information that I find about a particular topic into the document and read later. There is a great tool called Evernote (evernote.com) that you can cut and paste directly from a web page.

What should you sell? The real question is, what product or service can you do that people are already paying for?

If people are already paying for it why can't they pay you for the same product or service?

I know I'm making it sound really simple but it really is. If you're good at what to do, you take pride in your work, you get your work done when you say you will and you charge a fair price, why should they not want to pay you for your product or service.

Your job is to make yourself available to them.

We call that marketing.

Do This!-(5)

Use Google to research your specific products and services.

Objective:

Learn how to use simple search terms to research your business ideas.

Activity:

Use Google to research businesses similar to the one you would like to start.

Instructions: Page 43

A lot of people say "I can do so many things, which one should I choose?" I recommend taking the top three products and services that people are paying for and you have a passion for doing. Research how other companies are selling the same products and services.

I remember Mr. Brown, one of my dad's friends that he used to call every time something plumbing or electrical needed to be fixed. Mr. Brown worked for a plumbing and electrical company. I used to be so excited when he was coming over because Mr. Brown had tools for everything. I am certain that Mr. Brown had a lot of customers because of those tools. My point is that you have to at least look like you know what you are doing before you will ever get your first customer. I used this concept when I started my first business working on computers in people's homes. I would show up and take out all my tools before starting to work. Once people saw that I had the right tools they would relax and let me do what I came there to do.

7. Who will be my customers? Who will be my competition?

Who will be your customers? Your customers will be people that are already buying the product or service that you are selling. Your goal is to figure out how to get them to start spending their money with you.

Who will be your competition? You competition are the businesses that YOUR customers are already buying YOUR products and services from.

To answer these questions you must research your potential customers and competition to develop a marketing plan that will turn their customers into your customers.

Think about the things that make you choose to buy something from a particular vendor over another. Some people choose a vendor for their price others for their service. Others choose for the quality of the product or service.

You have to determine what your hook will be. Best price, best service, best quality or all three.

<table>
<tr><td>

Do This!-(6)

Who Are My Customers?

Objective:

Determine who will be the idea customer for your business.

Activity:

Use the Market Analysis worksheet to find out your customers and competition.

Instructions: Page 44

</td></tr>
</table>

A Few Questions to Ask?

- **?** Is my product or service: For males females or both
- **?** Is my product or service: For the old, young or both
- **?** Is my product or service: Used by a specific type of person

Chapter: 7. Who will be my customers? Who will be my competition?

21

- **?** Is my product or service: Something that needs to be sold face to face and/or online
- **?** Is my product or service: Something that only people that make over $$$$ can afford
- **?** Is my product or service: Something that makes life easier
- **?** Who are the businesses that my potential customers are already buying from
- **?** What do they like about them?

Do This!-(7)

Who is My Competition?

Objective:

Find out who your direct completion currently is.

Activity:

Use the **Competition Analysis** worksheet to record information about your competition.

Instructions: Page 47

8. How much should I charge?

How much should you charge? That depends on a number of factors. The first and most important factor is how much are people already paying for the same product or service. This will be how much your competition charges. You should have gotten this information in your research process.

The next important factor is how much you can afford to do it for and still make it worth your while. Just because people pay you to do something doesn't mean that you're actually making money.

Using Kevin as an example again, Kevin decides to charge $25 to cut each yard. Everyone else charges $50 to do the same yard. Kevin feels that he will get more business because he's charging less. What Kevin doesn't take into account is that by doing more yards for less money he is spending more money on gas to get to each account and actually perform the work. With gas prices the way they are today he could actually be losing money.

The most important factor is that you are able to charge more than it cost you to provide your product or service. Enough that makes it worth your while to do it.

One great piece of advice that I received from Sherman one of my mentors was "It doesn't matter how much you make, what matters is how much you keep". He said this while advising me on how much to charge and what to do with the money I received for my services.

My Uncle Harold who was a handyman that worked on air conditioners and heating units. One day we went to see Ms. Johnson who had a problem with her air conditioner that he had looked at the day prior to give her a quote on repairing the unit. She asked "Brother Andrews how much to fix it?" My uncle looked at me, and then said to her "$42.54". She then said "do it". I was so amazed the he could calculate to the penny. In the truck I asked "how did you know exactly how much to charge?" He said I didn't, but the giving that amount she perceived that I did so it was not up for debate.

9. How much will it cost to start my business?

There are a number of standard costs to legally set up a business. These costs along with the money that you would need to spend to buy the other items that will be needed are considered your startup costs.

The best thing to do at this point is to start documenting all the cost it will take to start your business. You can easily do this using either a startup budget template or create your own. It is best to use Microsoft's excel to work with his budget. **Some of the basic cost includes;**

- ➢ Incorporation with the State - $125
- ➢ Basic Website $500-$1000
- ➢ Business Cards $50 - $100
- ➢ Business Plan Development $0 - $700

Startup Budget
July 5, 2012

	Cash Needed to Start
Monthly Costs	
Salary of owner-manager	$6,000
All other salaries and wages	7,000
Rent	1,000
Advertising	2,000
Delivery expense	400
Supplies	500
Telephone	500
Other utilities	500
Insurance	600
Taxes, including social security	1,000
Interest	500
Maintenance	300
Legal and other professional fees	3,000
Miscellaneous	500
Subtotal	**$23,800**
One-Time Costs	
Fixtures and Equipment	$10,000
Decorating and remodeling	1,000
Installation charges	500
Starting inventory	5,000
Deposits with public utilities	1,000
Legal and other professional fees	500
Licenses and permits	500
Advertising and promotion for opening	500
Cash	750
Other	200
Subtotal	**$19,950**
Totals	**$43,750**

Do This!-(8)

Business Startup Budget

Objective:

Create a startup budget for your business.

Activity:

Use the budget worksheet to start listing cost for your business

Instructions: Page 52

10. How Do I Develop My Business Idea

Most people fail to spend the time necessary to develop the actual business idea. They jump right into working on the business plan or taking classes on starting a business. Some even get to the point of actually starting and running the business before they realize that maybe this particular idea was not the best one to start with.

It is very important to take time to research your business idea. The research can include using the internet, asking friends and family and even asking someone that you don't know who is doing what you want to do. You will be quickly surprised how open other business owners will be about the lessons learned while starting their business.

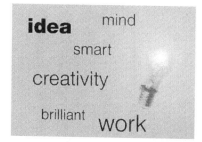

I recommend when approaching people to ask questions, keep your list of questions to a reasonable amount (5 to 6 questions). You may have more but be courteous of a person's time. You may want to call on them again. You don't want to overwhelm them. They might not respond when you call again.

One question to ask yourself,

Is this something that I would do if I did not need the money?

Most likely it will be rough going getting started. You WILL wake occasionally and ask yourself, "Why am I doing this?" You better have a good answer. (This is one of the few times it is ok to answer your own questions)

Don't spend weeks and weeks on this. Believe me you will continue to find out more as you move along the path. Put a start and stop date on this process. Say you are going to spend 1 or 2 weeks on this. If after this time you don't feel you have enough information, give yourself 1 additional week. Focus on only the things you still have questions about.

Do This!-(9)

Business Idea Creator

Objective

Develop the idea for 1 to 3 businesses.

Activity:

Complete the Business Idea Creator worksheet to help develop your business idea.

Instructions: Page 54

I promise that after you finish this process you will feel more confident about your idea.

 I have found that it is best to only work on your business idea with those that are directly involved in the business. You will find that all of a sudden everyone else becomes a business expert. They will have plenty of ideas and suggestions on how you should start your business. This will complicate your creative process because some of the ideas might be interesting. I suggest that you complete this on your own and then look for outside advice, preferably from someone that has actually done it.

11. How Do I Create an Action Plan to Start My Business

Yes we need another plan. You will need to develop an action plan that will help you stay on schedule as you develop a plan for your business. I call this a basic strategic plan for your business. It will help you keep all your task and ideas in one document that will be a living document as you develop your business ideas.

 It is important to develop this document so that you will stay on task and not be diverted by the new concepts and ideas as they present themselves to you. I recommend that you develop plans for 90 days at a time. This way you will not be overwhelmed and you can modify at 90 days intervals. There are consultants that teach workshops on this topic alone.

Use these guidelines when developing goals for your action plan;

Goals should always be: SMART

Do This!-(10)

Business Action Plan

Objective:

Create simple 90 day action plan for your business

Activity:

Use the Action Plan Worksheet to develop plan to start your business.

Instructions: Page 54

<u>S</u> – **Specific**-Don't be vague. Say exactly what you plan to do

<u>M</u> – **Measurable**-Make sure you can measure the success

<u>A</u> – **Achievable**-Choose goals that you are confident you can do

<u>R</u> – **Realistic**-Be reasonable. Don't create stress for yourself

<u>T</u> – **Time Bound**-Put down a date that you will complete the goal

12. Business Plan Assessment

Are you ready to answer a few questions about your business idea? Included in this book is the business plan assessment survey that I use when helping people write their business plans.

The survey covers the questions that you will answer when developing your plan. This is not a pass or fail survey. Some of the questions were not covered directly in this book, but you will need to start thinking about them before you start your plan. The goal of this survey is to make sure that you feel confident about your business idea and are ready to start working on your business plan.

The survey questions are divided into the sections that are in the standard business plan. You will be able to use these answers when working on your plan.

The sections are as follows;

- ➲ **Business Overview**- Covers the business type, purpose, reasons for starting, products/services and other general aspects of your business.

- ➲ **External Communications** – Covers how you will communicate to the world about your business.

- ➲ **Human Resources** – Covers how you will deal with hiring and managing the staff.

- ➲ **Products/Services** – Covers the products and/or services that your business will provide.

- ➲ **Marketing** – Covers how the business will be marketed.

- ➲ **Accounting/Financial** – Covers how you will handle the startup cost, accounting and financial aspects of your business.

The Business Development Assessment can be found at the end of the "Do This!" section of this book. The online survey instructions can also be found in this section.

Remember, this is not a pass or fail assessment. The purpose is to make sure that you understand and can answer these important questions.

Putting It All Together!

Now that you have completed the book and the associated exercises you should have a better understanding of what it will take to get your business started. I am sure that you now realize that there are even more questions to answer. Using the lessons learned in this book you now have the tools to research and find the answers.

What I want to you do now is to put all this information together into one place in preparation for working on a business plan. I promise that you will be very impressed with yourself once you review the total package.

Follow these steps

1. Get a 3 ring binder that has pockets to insert information that you might receive at a workshop or networking event.
2. Get a 3-hole punch that fits into the binder.
3. Put dividers in the binders that have 8 or more tabs.
4. Label the tabs as you would the sections in a business plan.
5. Print all the exercises that you completed in this book. If you used the worksheets in the book, copy the pages that contain the exercises. Do not remove them from the book.
6. Use the 3-hole punch to put holes in the documents.
7. Insert the documents into the sections that you feel they should go into the binder using the labels on the tabs.
8. Close the book and lay it down.
9. Find a comfortable place to sit and get your favorite beverage.
10. Start reading the book section by section and taking notes if needed.

I promise that you will be very impressed with the business idea described in the book

And that Business Idea is Yours!

Summary

Hopefully you now realize that you can start your own business if you follow a few basic steps. Remember, this is nothing new. We have been here before. There are people that you know that are doing it today. Reach out, go to a business networking event, and call people that you know. You will find that you are not much different than those that are out here building their lives and working hard for themselves.

The list below contains the major ideas that I want you to walk away with after reading this book.

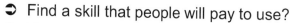

- ➲ That you must have the right mindset
- ➲ The real question is why should you not start your own business?
- ➲ Find a skill that people will pay to use?
- ➲ You are the product!
- ➲ Your customers will be people that are already buying the product or service that you are selling
- ➲ A business plan is needed to help guide you through the process of starting and running a business.
- ➲ The first three steps before starting a business are; RESEARCH, RESEARCH, RESEARCH
- ➲ How much can you afford to provide your product/service for and still make it worth your while?
- ➲ The best thing to do at this point is to start documenting all the cost it will take to start your business.
- ➲ You will need to develop an action plan that will help you stay on schedule as you develop a plan for your business
- ➲ And......

Yes You Can Do This!

Resource Websites

There are a number of great resources for helping you get your business started. You need to find a resource that best works for you. Some people need instructor led training while others prefer self-paced training. You might find that you like a little of both.

- The Capacity Builder Network
  - For-Profit Business   www.smallbusinesscapacitybuilder.com
  - Non-Profit Organization www.communitycapacitybuilders.org
- Research Sites
  - www.google.com
  - www.bing.com
  - www.ask.com
  - www.ezinearticles.com
- Bplans.com – Sample Business Plans
  - http://www.bplans.com/
- Small Business Administration
  - www.sba.gov
- Internal Revenue Service
  - www.irs.gov
- Informative Websites
  - http://entrepreneurs.about.com/
  - http://www.businessnewsdaily.com
  - http://www.startupsmart.com

Do You Need More Help?

My Business Coaching Program

I have been helping people start their businesses for a long time. Some people need to have someone helping them to stay focused and on task. I have developed a coaching package that will give you the opportunity to work directly with a business coach that will help you stay on track as you develop your plan for business.

The Basic Business Coaching Program Includes;

⊃ Online Workshops
⊃ Online Group Coaching Sessions
⊃ Membership to the Small Business Capacity Builder Network
⊃ Reduced price one-one coaching sessions
⊃ Document review
⊃ Online Forum Discussions
⊃ Get Questions Answered via Email
⊃ Access to Useful Online Tools

For more information about the Business Coaching Program

Go to www.capbuildernetwork.com and click on **Business Coaching** to view the program and request a FREE consultation.

Do This! Exercises

The exercises on the following pages relate back to the **"DoThis!"** side bars located throughout the book. These exercises will help you develop your ideas one piece at a time. Do the complete set of exercises for each business idea. Once all have been completed you will combine them together in preparation of developing a business plan.

The exercises may be completed one of three ways;

1. Fill out the forms included in this book
2. Download the PDF versions from the website
3. Do the exercises using the online surveys *(preferred)*

Do not mix the methods of completing the work

Using the exercises in the book

1. Try to make copies of each exercise before you use them or download the PDF versions from the Small Business Capacity Builder website using the instructions below
2. Complete each exercise by following the instructions

Download the PDF exercises

1. Go to the www.yesicanbookseries.com website
2. Select the **Do This! Exercises** menu tab from the menu
3. Select the link associated with the **Do This! PDF** Exercise that you want to download

Using the online exercises

NOTE: The password to all surveys is: **yesican** (all lowercase)

1. Go to the www.yesicanbookseries.com website
2. Select the **Do This! Exercise** menu tab from the menu
3. **Select the link** associated with the Do This! Exercise that you want to do
4. Enter the **password: yesican** to start the exercise

The online exercises are listed in the table below.

SPECIAL NOTE: You must enter the password: **yesican** to open each survey

Do This! Exercises: Online

DO THIS!	EXERCISE LINKS
1	Entrepreneurship Family Tree
2	Self-Assessment
3	Review Sample Business Plan
4	Research Your Business Idea
5	Research Your Products and Services
6	Who are my customers
7	Competition Analysis
8	Business Startup Budget
9	Business Idea Creator Survey
10	Business Action Plan
11	Business Plan Development Survey
11	Business Plan Survey - Background Information
11	Business Plan Survey - External Communications
11	Business Plan Survey - Marketing Strategy
11	Business Plan Survey - Products and Services
11	Business Plan Survey - Board of Advisors and Mentors
11	Business Plan Survey - Cost of Doing Business

Do This! (1) Entrepreneurship Family Tree
(Instructions for Online Exercises on Page 36)

If you take the time to think about it, there are many people that you know that have run some type of business. Some may have been a registered business others may have been a hobby or had a skill that people paid them to perform. The point is, generating revenue by using your own skills is not a new concept or reserved for people that have money or education. The one common trait is that they had passion for what they were doing and generally performed their work to the best of their ability.

Activity

Use the forms on the following pages to create a list of persons that you know living or deceased that have had their own business. For the sake of this exercise we will qualify a business as being;

A person providing a (legal) service or product to others and receiving payment

Let see what you come up with. I am certain that you will be pleasantly surprised.

Persons Name	Relationship	Type of Business
Your Comments		

Persons Name	Relationship	Type of Business
Your Comments		

Persons Name	Relationship	Type of Business
Your Comments		

Persons Name	Relationship	Type of Business
Your Comments		

Persons Name	Relationship	Type of Business
Your Comments		

Persons Name	Relationship	Type of Business
Your Comments		

Do This! (2) Self-Assessment
(Instructions for Online Exercises on Page 36)

This survey will ask you yes or no questions that pertain to some of the most important aspects of starting a business. This is not a pass or fail test. You will use the answer to determine what else you need to help you get started.

Once submitted you will receive a copy of your responses. Pay close attention to the "No" responses. These are the ones that we will need to focus on to get you ready for business.

Please provide the following (*required)

First Name* _____

Last Name* _____

Zip* _____

Phone* _____

Email* _____

General

1. DO YOU THINK YOU ARE READY TO START A BUSINESS?
(Select only one.)
- ☐ No
- ☐ Yes

2. HAVE YOU EVER WORKED IN A BUSINESS SIMILAR TO WHAT YOU ARE PLANNING TO START?
(Select only one.)
- ☐ No
- ☐ Yes

3. WOULD PEOPLE THAT KNOW YOU SAY YOU ARE WELL SUITED TO BE SELF-EMPLOYED?
(Select only one.)
- ☐ No
- ☐ Yes

4. Do you have support for your business from family and friends?

(Select only one.)

- ☐ No
- ☐ Yes

5. Have you ever taken a course or seminar designed to teach you how to start and manage a small business?

(Select only one.)

- ☐ No
- ☐ Yes

Personal Characteristics

6. Do you consider yourself a leader and self-starter?

(Select only one.)

- ☐ No
- ☐ Yes

7. Would other people consider you a leader?

(Select only one.)

- ☐ No
- ☐ Yes

8. Do you have enough confidence in yourself and your abilities to sustain yourself in business, if or when things get tough?

(Select only one.)

- ☐ No
- ☐ Yes

9. Do you like to make your own decisions?

(Select only one.)

- ☐ No
- ☐ Yes

10. Are you prepared, if needed, to temporarily lower your standard of living until your business is firmly established?

(Select only one.)

- ☐ No
- ☐ Yes

11. Are you willing to commit long hours to make your business work?

(Select only one.)

- ☐ No
- ☐ Yes

Skills and Experience

12. DO YOU HAVE A BUSINESS PLAN FOR THE BUSINESS YOU ARE PLANNING TO START?

(Select only one.)

☐ No

☐ Yes

13. DO YOU KNOW AND UNDERSTAND THE COMPONENTS OF A BUSINESS PLAN?

(Select only one.)

☐ No

☐ Yes

14. DO YOU KNOW WHAT FORM OF LEGAL OWNERSHIP (SOLE PROPRIETOR, PARTNERSHIP OR CORPORATION) IS BEST FOR YOUR BUSINESS?

(Select only one.)

☐ No

☐ Yes

15. DO YOU KNOW WHY SOME CONSIDER BUSINESS PLANNING TO BE THE MOST IMPORTANT FACTOR DETERMINING BUSINESS SUCCESS?

(Select only one.)

☐ No

☐ Yes

Additional Comments

16. PLEASE TELL WHY YOU FEEL THAT YOU ARE READY TO START A BUSINESS?

Do This! (3) Review Sample Business Plan
(Instructions for Online Exercises on Page 36)

The objective of this exercise is to learn how to research your business idea by reviewing the business plans of other businesses similar to your business idea.

A good start to finding sample business plans is to go to the website www.bplans.com.

The Blans.com website sells business plan software that assist with the development of a formal business plan. This site also contains many sample business plans that can be reviewed online.

Performing Research

There will be a lot of research using the internet that will be required for this and other exercises. One method for recording the information that you find interesting, is to copy and paste from the website to a Word or other word processing software.

As you come across interesting information, highlight it then copy and paste to the open document.

Instructions

Go to www.bplans.com

1. You may search for sample plans by 1 of 2 methods
2. Enter the type of business into the search field
3. Click on "Review Sample Plans" and follow the instructions from there
4. Select a plan to review
5. Click on the section of the plan in the menu window
6. Read each section of the plan to see if it is similar to what you would like to do
7. If you see something you like, highlight it, then copy and paste into the open word document.
8. Continue this process until you get the information you feel is important from this plan then move onto the next.

Do This! (4) Research Your Business Idea
(Instructions for Online Exercises on Page 36)

The objective of this exercise is to learn how to research your business idea by reviewing the websites of other businesses similar to your business idea.

One method of doing this is by using Google or another search engine (Bing, Ask, etc.) to search for specific information by using keywords or phrases.

Performing Research

There will be a lot of research using the internet that will be required for this and other exercises. One method for recording the information that you find interesting, is to copy and paste from the website to a Word or other word processing software.

As you come across interesting information, highlight it then copy and paste to the open document.

Instructions

1. Go to www.google.com
2. Enter a search term in the Search field (i.e. Landscape company, Day Care Center, etc.)
3. Click on the website link of something you find interesting
4. Review the site by clicking on the site menu tabs
5. If you see something you like, highlight it, then copy and paste into the open word document.
6. Continue this process until you get the information you feel is important from this page then move onto the next page or site

Do This! (5) Research Your Products and Services
(Instructions for Online Exercises on Page 36)

The objective of this exercise is to learn how to research your business idea by reviewing the websites that contain the products and services that you want to provide

One method of doing this is by using Google or another search engine (Bing, Ask, etc.) to search for specific information by using keywords or phrases.

Performing Research

There will be a lot of research using the internet that will be required for this and other exercises. One method for recording the information that you find interesting, is to copy and paste from the website to a Word or other word processing software.

As you come across interesting information, highlight it then copy and paste to the open document.

Instructions

1. Go to www.google.com
2. Enter a search term in the Search field (i.e. Tutoring, Cooking, cakes, barber, jewelry, etc.)
3. Click on the website link of something you find interesting
4. Review the site by clicking on the site menu tabs
5. If you see something you like, highlight it, then copy and paste into the open word document.
6. Continue this process until you get the information you feel is important from this page then move onto the next page or site

Do This! (6) Who Are My Customers?
(Instructions for Online Exercises on Page 36)

Answer questions as they relate to you. For most answers, check the boxes most applicable to you or fill in the blanks.

Please provide the following (*required)

First Name_____

Last Name_____

Title_____

Company_____

Address_____

City_____

State / Province_____

Postal Code_____

Phone_____

Email_____

Website_____

Survey Questions

1. WHAT IS THE AGE RANGE OF YOUR TARGET CUSTOMER?
   (Select all that apply.)
   ☐   0-9
   ☐   10-15
   ☐   16-25
   ☐   26-36
   ☐   37-50
   ☐   50 +

2. WHAT IS THE GENDER OF YOUR TARGET CUSTOMER?

☐ Male

☐ Female

☐ Other:

3. WHAT IS THE INCOME LEVEL OF YOUR TARGET CUSTOMER?

(Select all that apply.)

☐ 0-20,000

☐ 21,000-31,000

☐ 32,000-50,000

☐ 50,000-100,000

☐ 100,000 +

4. WHERE DOES YOUR TARGET CUSTOMER LIVE?

(Provide one response only.)

5. WHO DOES YOUR TARGET CUSTOMER BUY FROM NOW?

(Provide one response only.)

6. WHO ARE YOUR COMPETITORS?

(Provide one response only.)

7. HOW ARE THEIR PRICES COMPARED TO YOURS?

(Provide one response only.)

8. HOW IS THEIR CUSTOMER SERVICE COMPARED TO YOURS?

(Provide one response only.)

9. WHAT DO YOUR POTENTIAL CUSTOMERS THINK OF THEM?

(Provide one response only.)

10. WHAT IS THEIR GREATEST STRENGTH?
    (Provide one response only.)

11. WHAT IS THEIR KEY WEAKNESS?
    (Provide one response only.)

12. WHAT WILL YOUR BUSINESS SPECIFICALLY DO TO BEAT THE COMPETITION?
    (Provide one response only.)

Do This! (7) Competition Analysis
(Instructions for Online Exercises on Page 36)

This survey will be used for you to evaluate your competition. You will use the Internet to do research to perform a basic initial evaluation of your potential competition.

Please provide the following (*required)

First Name*_____

Last Name*_____

Company*_____

Address*_____

City*_____

State*_____

Zip*_____

Phone*_____

Email*_____

Competitive Analysis Business 1

1. BUSINESS 1 NAME

2. BUSINESS 1 PHONE NUMBER

3. BUSINESS 1 WEBSITE ADDRESS

4. RATE THE WEBSITE ON A SCALE OF 1 TO 5
   (Select only one.)
   ☐   1
   ☐   2
   ☐   3
   ☐   4
   ☐   5

5. BUSINESS (1) PRODUCT/SERVICE 1 (ENTER PRODUCT AND PRICING IF AVAILABLE)

6. BUSINESS (1) PRODUCT/SERVICE 2 (ENTER PRODUCT AND PRICING IF AVAILABLE)

7. BUSINESS (1) PRODUCT/SERVICE 3 (ENTER PRODUCT AND PRICING IF AVAILABLE)

8. LIST THE AREA SERVED

9. ENTER OTHER COMMENTS

Competitive Analysis Business 2

10. BUSINESS 2 NAME

11. BUSINESS 2 PHONE NUMBER

12. BUSINESS 2 WEBSITE ADDRESS

13. RATE THE WEBSITE ON A SCALE OF 1 TO 5
    (Select only one.)
    - ☐ 1
    - ☐ 2
    - ☐ 3
    - ☐ 4
    - ☐ 5

14. BUSINESS (2) PRODUCT/SERVICE 1 (ENTER PRODUCT AND PRICING IF AVAILABLE)

15. BUSINESS (2) PRODUCT/SERVICE 2 (ENTER PRODUCT AND PRICING IF AVAILABLE)

16. BUSINESS (2) PRODUCT/SERVICE 3 (ENTER PRODUCT AND PRICING IF AVAILABLE)

17. LIST THE AREA SERVED

18. ENTER OTHER COMMENTS

Competitive Analysis Business 3

19. BUSINESS 3 NAME

20. BUSINESS 3 PHONE NUMBER

21. BUSINESS 3 WEBSITE ADDRESS

22. RATE THE WEBSITE ON A SCALE OF 1 TO 5
    (Select only one.)
    ☐   1
    ☐   2
    ☐   3
    ☐   4
    ☐   5

23. BUSINESS (3) PRODUCT/SERVICE 1 (ENTER PRODUCT AND PRICING IF AVAILABLE)

24. BUSINESS (3) PRODUCT/SERVICE 2 (ENTER PRODUCT AND PRICING IF AVAILABLE)

25. BUSINESS (3) PRODUCT/SERVICE 3 (ENTER PRODUCT AND PRICING IF AVAILABLE)

26. LIST THE AREA SERVED

27. ENTER OTHER COMMENTS

Competitive Analysis Business 4

28. BUSINESS 4 NAME

29. BUSINESS 4 PHONE NUMBER

30. BUSINESS 4 WEBSITE ADDRESS

31. RATE THE WEBSITE ON A SCALE OF 1 TO 5
    (Select only one.)
    ☐   1
    ☐   2
    ☐   3
    ☐   4
    ☐   5

32. BUSINESS (4) PRODUCT/SERVICE 1 (ENTER PRODUCT AND PRICING IF AVAILABLE)

33. BUSINESS (4) PRODUCT/SERVICE 2 (ENTER PRODUCT AND PRICING IF AVAILABLE)

34. BUSINESS (4) PRODUCT/SERVICE 3 (ENTER PRODUCT AND PRICING IF AVAILABLE)

35. LIST THE AREA SERVED

36. ENTER OTHER COMMENTS

Do This! (8) Business Startup Budget
(Instructions for Online Exercises on Page 36)

The objective of this exercise is to figure out will it will cost to start and run your business.

There will be fixed cost or cost that will pretty much stay the same (i.e. rent, utilities, equipment, insurance, etc.). There also will be variable cost that will change as your business changes.

For example if you are starting a home painting business you might create a cost sheet for how much it will cost to paint an average 3 bedroom house. (I.e. paint, labor, supplies).

Instructions

1. Use the worksheet on the following page to start entering what the one time startup and the monthly ongoing cost will be.
   a. **NOTE:** *You may use estimates at this point. The actual cost will be finalized later.*
2. Some of the types of cost are already entered. There are blank spaces for you to add your own.
3. Enter all the cost and then total each section;
   a. **Monthly Ongoing**
   b. **On Time Startup**
4. The total of these two sections will give you the total estimated startup cost.

Startup Budget

	Cash Needed to Start	COMMENT
Monthly Costs		
Salary of owner-manager		
Labor		
Rent		
Advertising (Webhosting, etc.)		
Telephone and Internet		
Office supplies		
Travel		
Miscellaneous		
Subtotal		

	Cash Needed to Start	COMMENT
One-Time Costs		
Incorporate with State		
Business License		
Equipment and tools		
Marketing - Website Setup		
Marketing - Business cards, Flyers		
Legal and other professional fees		
Licenses and permits		
Advertising and promotion for opening		
Cash		
Cash		
Other		
Subtotal		

Do This! (9) Business Idea Creator
(Instructions for Online Exercises on Page 36)

This survey will help you to come up with your business ideas. The results from this survey will give you the items that you will need to do research on. Do not think too deeply about your answers. Answer questions as they relate to you. For most answers, check the boxes most applicable to you or fill in the blanks.

Please provide the following (*required)

First Name*_____

Last Name*_____

Zip*_____

Phone*_____

Email*_____

Basic Questions

1. WHAT TYPE OF BUSINESS DO YOU WANT TO START?

2. WHY WILL YOU BE SUCCESSFUL WITH THIS TYPE OF BUSINESS? (YOU HAVE A CERTAIN SKILL, BACKGROUND, EXPERIENCE AND/OR PASSION FOR THIS TYPE OF BUSINESS)

3. WHEN WILL YOU START YOUR BUSINESS? (LETS PUT A LINE IN THE SAND. PICK A TIME THAT YOU PLAN TO GET YOUR BUSINESS GOING)

Business Idea Questions

4. WHAT WILL YOUR BUSINESS DO? (FOR EXAMPLE, START WITH "WE PROVIDE")

5. WHAT ARE YOUR TOP 3 PRODUCTS OR SERVICES THAT YOU WILL OFFER?

6. WHO IS YOUR COMPETITION?

7. WHO WILL BUY YOUR PRODUCTS AND SERVICES?

8. WHY WILL THEY BUY IT FROM YOU?

9. HOW WILL YOU SELL YOUR PRODUCT/SERVICE?
   (Select all that apply.)
   ☐   Person to Person
   ☐   Person to Business
   ☐   Business to Business
   ☐   In a Store
   ☐   Online using the Internet
   ☐   Other:

10. WHERE WILL YOU GET THE FUNDING TO START YOUR BUSINESS?

(Select all that apply.)

- ☐ Friends
- ☐ Family
- ☐ Business Loan
- ☐ Credit Card
- ☐ SBA
- ☐ Micro Lender

11. WHERE CAN YOU GO FOR HELP?

(Select all that apply.)

- ☐ Small Business Capacity Builder
- ☐ Community Capacity Builder
- ☐ SBA.GOV
- ☐ SCORE
- ☐ Urban League
- ☐ Other:

12. PLEASE ENTER ANY ADDITIONAL COMMENTS.

Do This! (10) Business Action Plan
(Instructions for Online Exercises on Page 36)

Company Information

Company Name: _____

Contact Name: _____

Phone: _____   Email : _____

Website: _____

Date: _____   Time Period: **to**

Instructions

Goals should always be: **S** – Specific   **M** – Measurable   **A** – Achievable   **R** – Realistic   **T** – Time Bound

Use the descriptions below to fill in the Business Goal Activity Planning worksheets. You might do this more than once for the same goal. The objective is to get you to start thinking through and creating the task to achieve your goals. This can be used for more than your business.

3 Business Goal Activity Planning worksheets are included with this template. Just copy these worksheets if you need more.

1. **Goal/Objective:** Briefly describe each goal/objective and when the goal/objective should be met or accomplished.
2. **Rewards**: What will be the potential rewards for the completion of the goal
3. **Consequences**: What will be the potential consequences if the goal is not completed
4. **Prerequisite Goal:** Any goal that must be completed before the activities of this goal can start.
5. **Possible Obstacles**: What are some of the potential obstacles that will possibly hinder the successful completion of this goal?
6. **Action Steps**: What are the actions steps needed to complete this goal
7. **Date Due**: When is this goal to be completed
8. **Who**: Who is responsible or will be needed for completing this goal
9. **Date Completed**: What is the date this goal was actually completed.

Business Goal Activity Planning

Goal Description	
Rewards	
Consequences	
Prerequisite Goal	

Action Steps

ID	Possible Obstacles	Action Steps	Date Due	Who	Date Comp

Business Goal Activity Planning

Goal Description	
Rewards	
Consequences	
Prerequisite Goal	

Action Steps

ID	Possible Obstacles	Action Steps	Date Due	Who	Date Comp

Business Goal Activity Planning

Goal Description	
Rewards	
Consequences	
Prerequisite Goal	

Action Steps

I D	Possible Obstacles	Action Steps	Date Due	Who	Date Comp

Business Goal Activity Planning

Goal Description	
Rewards	
Consequences	
Prerequisite Goal	

Action Steps

ID	Possible Obstacles	Action Steps	Date Due	Who	Date Comp

Business Goal Activity Planning

Goal Description	
Rewards	
Consequences	
Prerequisite Goal	

Action Steps

I D	Possible Obstacles	Action Steps	Date Due	Who	Date Comp

Do This! (11) Business Development Assessment
(Instructions for Online Exercises on Page 36)

The following questions are basic questions about your business. The questions will help you define the purpose and structure for your business. Answer questions as they relate to you. For most answers, check the boxes most applicable to you or fill in the blanks.

Please provide the following (*required)

First Name_____

Last Name_____

Title_____

Organization_____

Address_____

City_____

State_____

Zip_____

Phone_____

Email_____

Website_____

Business Overview

1. WHAT TYPE OF BUSINESS DO YOU HAVE OR PLAN TO DEVELOP?
   (Provide one response only.)

2. WHAT IS THE PURPOSE OF THIS BUSINESS?
   (Provide one response only.)

3. WHAT IS THE KEY MESSAGE OR PHRASE TO DESCRIBE YOUR BUSINESS IN ONE SENTENCE?
   (Provide one response only.)

4. WHAT IS YOUR REASON FOR STARTING YOUR OWN BUSINESS?
   (Provide one response only.)

5. WHAT IS YOUR PRODUCT OR SERVICE?
   (Provide one response only.)

6. IS YOUR PRODUCT OR SERVICE USED IN CONNECTION WITH OTHER PRODUCTS OR SERVICES?
   (Provide one response only.)

7. WHAT LED YOU TO DEVELOP YOUR PRODUCT OR SERVICE?
   (Provide one response only.)

8. WHEN WILL YOUR PRODUCT BE AVAILABLE?
   (Provide one response only.)

9. WHAT TYPE OF CORPORATE STRUCTURE IS/WILL YOUR BUSINESS BE?

(Select only one.)

- ☐ C-Corporation
- ☐ S-Corporation
- ☐ Non-Profit
- ☐ Limited Liability Corporation
- ☐ Sole-Proprietor

10. HAVE YOU FILLED YOUR CORPORATION PAPERS WITH THE GOVERNMENT?

(Select only one.)

- ☐ Yes
- ☐ No
- ☐ Other:

11. IF YOU HAVE FILLED YOUR CORPORATION PAPERS, WHEN WAS THIS DONE?

(Provide one response only.)

12. DO YOU HAVE THE MANAGEMENT TEAM NEEDED TO ACHIEVE YOUR GOALS?

(Select only one.)

- ☐ Yes
- ☐ No
- ☐ Other:

13. PLEASE DESCRIBE THE MANAGEMENT TEAM

(Provide one response only.)

14. PLEASE ADD ANY OTHER COMMENTS THAT YOU FEEL IMPORTANT

(Provide one response only.)

External Communications / Info Production and Dissemination / Networking

15. DO YOU HAVE DATA SHEETS, BROCHURES, DIAGRAMS, SKETCHES, PHOTOGRAPHS, RELATED PRESS RELEASES OR OTHER DOCUMENTATION ABOUT YOUR PRODUCT/SERVICE?
(Provide one response only.)

16. WHO DO YOU NEED TO BE COMMUNICATING WITH MORE?
(Provide one response only.)

17. DO YOU PUBLISH YOUR OWN PRESS RELEASES, NEWS BULLETINS, NEWSLETTERS, BROCHURES, FLYERS, EMAIL ALERTS, ETC?
(Select only one.)
- ☐ Yes
- ☐ No
- ☐ Other:

18. ARE THE PUBLICATIONS IN PRINTED OR ONLINE FORMAT?
(Select only one.)
- ☐ Online
- ☐ Printed
- ☐ Both

19. WHO WRITES CONTENT FOR THE PRESS RELEASES, NEWSLETTERS, ETC.?
(Provide one response only.)

20. DO YOU HAVE ANY CONTACTS WITH THE LOCAL PRESS? HAVE THERE BEEN ARTICLES WRITTEN ABOUT YOUR ORGANIZATION OR PUBLISHED IN OUTSIDE SOURCES?
(Select only one.)
- ☐ Yes
- ☐ No
- ☐ Explain:

21. DO YOU HAVE OR HAVE EVER USED THE SERVICES OF A PUBLICIST FOR MEDIA RELATIONS OR MEDIA DEVELOPMENT?

(Select only one.)

- ☐ Yes
- ☐ No
- ☐ Explain:

22. DO YOU HAVE ANY OTHER PROMOTIONAL MATERIALS – BROCHURES, ANNUAL REPORT, ETC

(Select only one.)

- ☐ Yes
- ☐ No
- ☐ Other:

23. DO YOU HAVE A MARKETING PLAN, PROPOSAL, STRATEGY OR ONE-SHEET?

(Select only one.)

- ☐ Yes
- ☐ No
- ☐ Other:

24. IF YES TO ABOVE QUESTION, HOW OFTEN ARE THESE DEVELOPED, IMPLEMENTED, AND/OR ASSESSED?

(Provide one response only.)

25. IS YOUR BRAND SOLIDIFIED – DO PEOPLE ASSOCIATE YOUR MISSION, PURPOSE, OBJECTIVES, LOGO, ORGANIZATION'S COLORS OR WEBSITE TO YOUR BUSINESS NAME?

(Select only one.)

- ☐ Yes
- ☐ No
- ☐ Explain:

26. DO YOU UNDERSTAND THE PURPOSE OF BRANDING?

(Select only one.)

- ☐ Yes
- ☐ Explain:

27. PLEASE ADD ANY ADDITIONAL COMMENTS

(Provide one response only.)

Human Resources

28. DO YOU HAVE A HUMAN RESOURCE PERSON ON STAFF?

(Select only one.)

☐   Yes

☐   No

☐   Explain:

29. DO YOU HAVE STANDARD HUMAN RESOURCE POLICES AND PROCEDURES?

(Select only one.)

☐   Yes

☐   No

☐   Explain:

30. DO YOU HAVE DOCUMENTATION FOR HIRING AND FIRING STAFF AND OTHER PERSONNEL?

(Select only one.)

☐   Yes

☐   No

☐   Explain:

31. DO YOU HAVE A STANDARD OPERATING PLAN?

(Select only one.)

☐   Yes

☐   No

☐   Explain:

Products / Services

32. WHAT IS THE PRODUCT APPLICATION? HOW WILL THE PRODUCT OR SERVICE BE USED?

(Provide one response only.)

33. CAN YOU LIST THREE UNIQUE BENEFITS OF YOUR PRODUCT OR SERVICE?

(Provide one response only.)

34. WHAT IS THE PRICING OF YOUR PRODUCT VERSUS YOUR COMPETITION?

(Provide one response only.)

35. DO YOU HAVE AN INVENTORY MANAGEMENT SYSTEM OR PROCEDURES IN PLACE?
   (Select only one.)
   ☐   Yes
   ☐   No
   ☐   Explain:

36. PLEASE ADD ANY OTHER COMMENTS THAT YOU FEEL IMPORTANT
   (Provide one response only.)

Marketing

37. WHO IS YOUR TARGET AUDIENCE?
   (Provide one response only.)

38. WHO IS YOUR COMPETITION?
   (Provide one response only.)

39. HOW IS YOUR PRODUCT DIFFERENTIATED FROM THAT OF YOUR COMPETITION?
   (Provide one response only.)

40. HAVE YOU DEVELOPED A MARKETING PLAN?
   (Select only one.)
   ☐   Yes
   ☐   No
   ☐   Other:

41. LIST THE TOP THREE OBJECTIONS TO BUYING YOUR PRODUCT/SERVICE IMMEDIATELY?
   (Provide one response only.)

42. PLEASE ADD ANY OTHER COMMENTS THAT YOU FEEL IMPORTANT
   (Provide one response only.)

Accounting/Financial Information

43. HAVE YOU DEVELOPED A BUDGET FOR THE BUSINESS?
(Select only one.)
- ☐ Yes
- ☐ No
- ☐ Other:

44. DO YOU USE AN ACCOUNTING SYSTEM?
(Select only one.)
- ☐ Yes
- ☐ Other:

45. IF YOU DO USE AN ACCOUNTING SYSTEM PLEASE LIST THE NAME AND VERSION NUMBER.
(Provide one response only.)

46. HOW WILL YOU FINANCE COMPANY GROWTH?
(Select all that apply.)
- ☐ Loans from private sources
- ☐ Self Finance
- ☐ Investors
- ☐ Loans from banks
- ☐ Loans from the government
- ☐ Other:

47. DO YOU HAVE ANY IMMEDIATE FINANCIAL NEEDS?
(Select only one.)
- ☐ Yes
- ☐ No
- ☐ Other:

48. DO YOU HAVE OR WORK WITH A CPA?
(Select only one.)
- ☐ Yes
- ☐ No
- ☐ Other:

49. HAVE YOU FILED LAST YEARS TAX RETURN?
(Select only one.)

- ☐   Yes
- ☐   No
- ☐   Explain:

50. PLEASE ADD ANY ADDITIONAL COMMENTS
(Provide one response only.)

Marc E. Parham has been successfully consulting for all types of businesses for over 20 years. He has consulted for small to mid-sized business, large corporations, and non-profit organizations in all areas of business development. He has certifications in Project management, Network Engineering, Non-profit Management and other areas of business development. Marc has made it his mission to help people start and grow their small businesses. He has created a successful business coaching program that has assisted many people in changing their lives. He is also available for speaking and training events. Please use the contact information below.

Marc E. Parham

Website: www.partecgroup.com
Email: marcp@partecgroup.com
Linkedin: marcp@partecgroup.com
Twitter: www.twitter.com/MarcEParham
Website: www.marceparham.com

For more information about the **Partec Consulting Group** *and other informative articles please go to www.partecgroup.com*

To learn more about **starting and growing your small business**

Go to www.capbuildernetwork.com

Made in the USA
Charleston, SC
29 April 2013